You Are Different.

You are Special.

By: Jessica Marie Benson

To My Dear Sweet Chase Patrick,

My little monkey.

My first born love.

My hero.

My special little boy.

*To anyone who is lucky enough
to be different,*

YOU ARE SPECIAL!

He was always different
and set himself apart.
His mommy said he's special.
She meant it from her heart.

Sometimes his voice got louder
or repeated things he said.
Sometimes he can't control the
thoughts running through his head.

His mommy said "Sometimes we're
quiet and sometimes we get loud.
But you try your hardest little one.
You just stand out from the crowd".

Sometimes he preferred to be alone.
He wasn't being mean.
Often crowds would make him scared
and he would cry or cause a scene.

His mommy would just hold him
until his fear was through.
"Don't worry if they're looking.
Just pretend it's me and you".

Sometimes he liked to jump about
like he was overcome with joy.
He gets excited for no reason.
"My special little boy".

Sometimes he would fidget.
Sometimes he'd run around.
Sometimes his arms would flap about
and he'd have trouble calming down.

His mommy said "I know it's hard"
and kissed him on the cheek.
"But we can work on sitting still.
You are special. You're unique".

Sometimes he would giggle
when there wasn't even a joke.
But his laughter was contagious
and smiles he'd provoke.

His mommy told him "It's okay,
It's always good to smile.
But there are times that we calm down
and be quiet for a while".

Sometimes he'd start to cry a bit
when he wasn't really sad,
and people would confuse this
with signs of being bad.

But he's not bad. He's special.
His mommy tells him so.
"Don't let anyone tell you different.
Sometimes they just don't know".

Sometimes he may wander off.
Sometimes he'll try to run.
His mommy says "Stay close to me.
My special little son".

"I know you try to listen
and you try your hardest to be good.
I will also try my best.
I wouldn't change things if I could".

He may not always hug you
or look you in the eye.
Sometimes you'll think he doesn't hear
and sometimes he'll act shy.

Sometimes he can not focus
or pay attention from the start.
His mommy tells him "I know you.
You are special. You are smart".

"Some can't understand these things
and have many questions why,
but don't you let that bring you down.
My special little guy".

It's hard for him to understand
how people need their space.
He may like to sit real close
or talk right to your face.

Sometimes he's too excited to talk
to those he likes so much.
His mommy says "Move back a bit.
You don't always have to touch".

People give him funny looks
and sometimes they will stare.
His mommy tells him "It's okay.
A boy like you is rare".

"Sometimes, people, they will judge and won't always understand.
But mommy is always on your side.
I'll be there to hold your hand".

Some people find it hard to grasp,
A way they can not be.
You're not just different. You are special.
And you are perfect to me".